MW01624236

this book belongs to

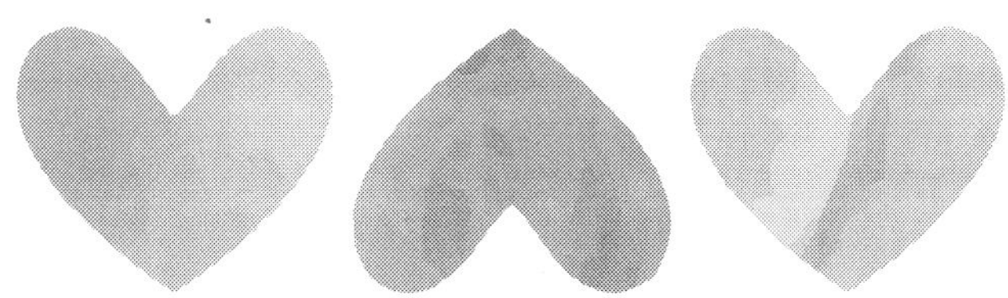

KISSING BOOKS

a journal for romance readers

HeartEyes Press

Published by Heart Eyes Press.

table of contents

book tracker

a space to fill in 200 books you've read, or maybe your TBR pile

LISTS

auto-buy authors

LISTS

recent five star reads

"I would buy their grocery list!"

LISTS

gems to recommend

LISTS

new to-me authors

"Read it or we're not friends."

all star wall

best cover
best animal friend
best heroine
best setting
best omg moment
best hero

my tbr

a place to list books you want to read, but don't have the time for yet.

❑ ____________________ BY: ____________________

❑ ____________________ BY: ____________________

❑ ____________________ BY: ____________________

❑ ____________________ BY: ____________________

❑ ____________________ BY: ____________________

❑ ____________________ BY: ____________________

❑ ____________________ BY: ____________________

❑ ____________________ BY: ____________________

❑ ____________________ BY: ____________________

❑ ____________________ BY: ____________________

❑ ____________________ BY: ____________________

❑ ____________________ BY: ____________________

❑ ____________________ BY: ____________________

❑ ____________________ BY: ____________________

❑ ____________________ BY: ____________________

❑ ____________________ BY: ____________________

❑ ____________________ BY: ____________________

❑ ____________________ BY: ____________________

❑ ____________________ BY: ____________________

❑ ____________________ BY: ____________________

❑ ____________________ BY: ____________________

❑ ____________________ BY: ____________________

❑ ____________________ BY: ____________________

❑ ____________________ BY: ____________________

❑ ____________________ BY: ____________________

❑ ______ BY: ______

❑ ______ BY: ______

❑ ______ BY: ______

❑ ______ BY: ______

❑ ______ BY: ______

❑ ______ BY: ______

❑ ______ BY: ______

❑ ______ BY: ______

❑ ______ BY: ______

❑ ______ BY: ______

❑ ______ BY: ______

❑ ______ BY: ______

❑ ______ BY: ______

❑ ______ BY: ______

❑ ______ BY: ______

❑ ______ BY: ______

❑ ______ BY: ______

❑ ______ BY: ______

❑ ______ BY: ______

❑ ______ BY: ______

❑ ______ BY: ______

❑ ______ BY: ______

❑ ______ BY: ______

❑ ______ BY: ______

❑ ______ BY: ______

more tbr

a place to list even more books you want to read, but don't have the time for yet.

- ❑ ______ BY: ______
- ❑ ______ BY: ______
- ❑ ______ BY: ______
- ❑ ______ BY: ______
- ❑ ______ BY: ______
- ❑ ______ BY: ______
- ❑ ______ BY: ______
- ❑ ______ BY: ______
- ❑ ______ BY: ______
- ❑ ______ BY: ______
- ❑ ______ BY: ______
- ❑ ______ BY: ______
- ❑ ______ BY: ______
- ❑ ______ BY: ______
- ❑ ______ BY: ______
- ❑ ______ BY: ______
- ❑ ______ BY: ______
- ❑ ______ BY: ______
- ❑ ______ BY: ______
- ❑ ______ BY: ______
- ❑ ______ BY: ______
- ❑ ______ BY: ______
- ❑ ______ BY: ______
- ❑ ______ BY: ______
- ❑ ______ BY: ______

- [ ] BY:
- [ ] BY:
- [ ] BY:
- [ ] BY:
- [ ] BY:
- [ ] BY:
- [ ] BY:
- [ ] BY:
- [ ] BY:
- [ ] BY:
- [ ] BY:
- [ ] BY:
- [ ] BY:
- [ ] BY:
- [ ] BY:
- [ ] BY:
- [ ] BY:
- [ ] BY:
- [ ] BY:
- [ ] BY:
- [ ] BY:
- [ ] BY:
- [ ] BY:
- [ ] BY:
- [ ] BY:

ROMANCE BINGO

summer edition!

Snarky Main Character	*Romantic comedy*	Friends to lovers	**New-to-me author**	I pre-ordered it
Illustrated cover	*It's lust at first sight*	**Read it on vacation**	Brown-eyed main character	*Body-positive story*
Letting out a breath they didn't know they were holding	**Neighbors**	**FREE SPACE**	**Main character rides a motorcycle**	**Romantic comedy**
One night stand	**Party scene**	*Historical romance*	**Flower(s) are on the cover**	**Sports romance**
Made me LOL!	**Cover is (mostly) blue**	Beach scene	**Outdoor nookie**	Main character is over 35

ROMANCE BINGO

fall edition!

Main character has a tattoo	**Bathtub or shower nookie**	Love at first sight	**Witty main character**	*Fake relationship*
Someone calls the police	Main character gets married	**Sequel**	**Bad boy or bad girl**	Animal on the cover
A smile that doesn't reach their eyes	**Friends to lovers**	**FREE SPACE**	Shirtless cover	*Published this year*
Cover is (mostly) yellow	Gray-eyed main character	**Childhood friends**	*Set in a small town*	**Takes place in the fall**
Workplace romance	**I won it**	*Romantic comedy*	**Shopping scene**	Tear-jerker

ROMANCE BINGO

winter edition!

Billionaire main character	**Hospital scene**	Main characters are snowed in	**Virgin main character**	*Made me cry*
Chose it for the cover	Character has a pet	**Made me laugh**	*Holiday romance*	**Borrowed it from my library**
I bought the book on sale	**Awful parent(s)**	**FREE SPACE**	I read it in paperback	**Set in a big city**
Blue-eyed main character	*Published at least 5 years ago*	Bar or tavern scene	**Main character wears glasses**	**Made me blush**
Shirtless man on the cover	**Amazing writing**	*Enemies to lovers*	**Single parent**	Set in a country you have never been

ROMANCE BINGO

spring edition!

First book in a series	**Main character is a nerd**	*I'm on the author's mailing list*	**Cover is (mostly) pink**	*Main character has a horse*
Friends to lovers	**Published this year**	Bought it on sale	**Main character is under 22**	Main character has an awful ex
Second chance at love	*Green-eyed main character*	**FREE SPACE**	Accidental pregnancy	**It was recommended to me**
Amazing twist	**LGBTQ characters**	Only one bed	**Animal on the cover**	*Takes place in the spring*
Made me laugh	Main character was a player	**Couple on the cover**	Unusual jobs	Friends to lovers

romance acronyms

HEA & HFN
Happily Ever After and Happy For Now. IE: #goals

CR
Contemporary Romance

P/O
Pre-order. See: causes of the TBR.

DNF
Did Not Finish. IE: sadly not worthy.

F2L
Friends to lovers. Like When Harry Met Sally, but sexier. #goals

M/F M/M F/F M/F MMF MFM
Male / Female, Male / Male, Female / Female. & all the glorious combinations therein.

RS
Romantic Suspense. IE: someone is imperiled and the alpha and several badass friends are there to save the day

MCs
Main Characters. IE: those people who make us laugh and cry.

DIK
Desert Island Keeper. IE: a book you could read forever and still love it

PNR
Paranormal Romance IE: witches, vampires, werewolves or werehamsters, etc

TSTL
Too stupid to live. IE when the hero or heroine makes mistakes so vast you shout at the page

TBR
To Be Read. IE: that towering stack of books we all have because we are weak in the face of a sale.

BDSM
Stands for Bondage, Dominance, Submission and Masochism, depending on who you ask. For further reference, ask Christian Grey

YA
Young Adult. IE: characters in high school

NA
New Adult. IE: characters in college, possibly drunk

romance jargon

Alphahole
A hero who is so alpha he sweats testosterone, speaks with words that prolly lack an endin' and bosses the heroine around way too much. Yet he's still sexy AF. AKA a man who's sometimes acceptable in a romance novel but you'd want to avoid IRL.

Cinnamon Roll
A hero who's spicy on the outside but sweet and gooey on the inside.

Instalove
They both reach for the same grapefruit at the grocery store, and there are hearts in their eyes forever after.

The Dark Moment
When absolutely everything goes wrong, and your couple can't be together, possibly because the hero has been a dickweasel and even his dog hates him.

Binge
To inhale a series when you are supposed to be doing something else. Like making a living, or folding your damn laundry.

Archetype
A familiar character role, like the protective bodyguard hero, or the cocky professional athlete. Basically, the human equivalent of a trope.

Doormat
A heroine who needs to grow a backbone immediately. Hopefully she does this before the epilogue. We're pulling for her.

Beta
A hero who does not have alphahole tendencies. He's a mild-mannered kind of sexy and does not need to fight the heroine at every turn.

Autobuy/Grocery List/One Click Authors
This is an author whose book you'll preorder without reading the description. If she published her grocery list, you'd probably buy that, too.

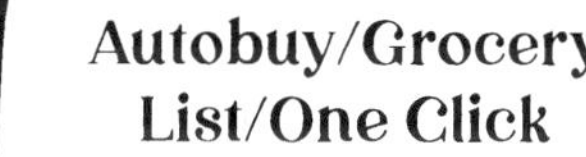

Catnip
That trope/archetype /setup you can never resist. Like secret babies, or heroes who fight fires for a living, or single dads.

Trope
A familiar setup or storyline, like enemies-to-lovers, or married-in-Vegas, or one-night-stand, or hot-for-teacher. Most romance novels are based on one or more familiar tropes. But if you tell us that makes romance formulaic, we will cut you.

Grumpy vs Sunshine
One of our characters is a grump (with excellent reasons) but he or she just can't help being attracted to his or her more sunshiny counterpart.

"I shall be miserable if I have not an excellent library."

JANE AUSTEN

book review notes

Title:

AUTHOR:

SERIES/GENRE:

DATE STARTED

DATE FINISHED

EBOOK PAPER AUDIO

MY RATING

❑ REVIEWED?

GREAT: CHARACTERS PLOT SUSPENSE DRAMA HUMOR HEROINE HERO ORIGINALITY ANGST EMOTIONS DIALOGUE ACTION WIT BANTER SEX SCENES SETTING DETAIL CONFLICT BACKSTORY

2

Title:

AUTHOR:

SERIES/GENRE:

DATE STARTED

DATE FINISHED

EBOOK PAPER AUDIO

MY RATING

❑ REVIEWED?

GREAT: CHARACTERS PLOT SUSPENSE DRAMA HUMOR HEROINE HERO ORIGINALITY ANGST EMOTIONS DIALOGUE ACTION WIT BANTER SEX SCENES SETTING DETAIL CONFLICT BACKSTORY

Title:

AUTHOR: ____________________

SERIES/GENRE: ____________________

DATE STARTED

DATE FINISHED

EBOOK PAPER AUDIO

MY RATING

❑ REVIEWED?

GREAT: CHARACTERS PLOT SUSPENSE DRAMA HUMOR HEROINE HERO ORIGINALITY ANGST EMOTIONS DIALOGUE ACTION WIT BANTER SEX SCENES SETTING DETAIL CONFLICT BACKSTORY

Title:

AUTHOR: ____________________

SERIES/GENRE: ____________________

DATE STARTED

DATE FINISHED

EBOOK PAPER AUDIO

MY RATING

❑ REVIEWED?

GREAT: CHARACTERS PLOT SUSPENSE DRAMA HUMOR HEROINE HERO ORIGINALITY ANGST EMOTIONS DIALOGUE ACTION WIT BANTER SEX SCENES SETTING DETAIL CONFLICT BACKSTORY

Title:

AUTHOR:

SERIES/GENRE:

DATE STARTED

DATE FINISHED

EBOOK PAPER AUDIO

MY RATING

❑ REVIEWED?

GREAT: CHARACTERS PLOT SUSPENSE DRAMA HUMOR HEROINE HERO ORIGINALITY ANGST EMOTIONS DIALOGUE ACTION WIT BANTER SEX SCENES SETTING DETAIL CONFLICT BACKSTORY

Title:

AUTHOR:

SERIES/GENRE:

DATE STARTED

DATE FINISHED

EBOOK PAPER AUDIO

MY RATING

❑ REVIEWED?

GREAT: CHARACTERS PLOT SUSPENSE DRAMA HUMOR HEROINE HERO ORIGINALITY ANGST EMOTIONS DIALOGUE ACTION WIT BANTER SEX SCENES SETTING DETAIL CONFLICT BACKSTORY

Title:

AUTHOR:

SERIES/GENRE:

DATE STARTED

DATE FINISHED

EBOOK PAPER AUDIO

MY RATING

☐ REVIEWED?

GREAT: CHARACTERS PLOT SUSPENSE DRAMA HUMOR HEROINE HERO ORIGINALITY ANGST EMOTIONS DIALOGUE ACTION WIT BANTER SEX SCENES SETTING DETAIL CONFLICT BACKSTORY

Title:

AUTHOR:

SERIES/GENRE:

DATE STARTED

DATE FINISHED

EBOOK PAPER AUDIO

MY RATING

☐ REVIEWED?

GREAT: CHARACTERS PLOT SUSPENSE DRAMA HUMOR HEROINE HERO ORIGINALITY ANGST EMOTIONS DIALOGUE ACTION WIT BANTER SEX SCENES SETTING DETAIL CONFLICT BACKSTORY

Title:

AUTHOR: ____

DATE STARTED

SERIES/GENRE: ____

DATE FINISHED

EBOOK PAPER AUDIO

MY RATING

GREAT: CHARACTERS PLOT SUSPENSE DRAMA HUMOR HEROINE HERO ORIGINALITY ANGST EMOTIONS DIALOGUE ACTION WIT BANTER SEX SCENES SETTING DETAIL CONFLICT BACKSTORY

❑ REVIEWED?

10

Title:

AUTHOR: ____

DATE STARTED

SERIES/GENRE: ____

DATE FINISHED

EBOOK PAPER AUDIO

MY RATING

GREAT: CHARACTERS PLOT SUSPENSE DRAMA HUMOR HEROINE HERO ORIGINALITY ANGST EMOTIONS DIALOGUE ACTION WIT BANTER SEX SCENES SETTING DETAIL CONFLICT BACKSTORY

❑ REVIEWED?

Title:

AUTHOR:

SERIES/GENRE:

DATE STARTED

DATE FINISHED

EBOOK PAPER AUDIO

MY RATING

❑ REVIEWED?

GREAT: CHARACTERS PLOT SUSPENSE DRAMA HUMOR HEROINE HERO ORIGINALITY ANGST EMOTIONS DIALOGUE ACTION WIT BANTER SEX SCENES SETTING DETAIL CONFLICT BACKSTORY

Title:

AUTHOR:

SERIES/GENRE:

DATE STARTED

DATE FINISHED

EBOOK PAPER AUDIO

MY RATING

❑ REVIEWED?

GREAT: CHARACTERS PLOT SUSPENSE DRAMA HUMOR HEROINE HERO ORIGINALITY ANGST EMOTIONS DIALOGUE ACTION WIT BANTER SEX SCENES SETTING DETAIL CONFLICT BACKSTORY

Title:

AUTHOR:

SERIES/GENRE:

DATE STARTED

/ /

DATE FINISHED

/ /

EBOOK PAPER AUDIO

MY RATING

☆ ☆ ☆ ☆ ☆

GREAT: CHARACTERS PLOT SUSPENSE DRAMA HUMOR HEROINE HERO ORIGINALITY ANGST EMOTIONS DIALOGUE ACTION WIT BANTER SEX SCENES SETTING DETAIL CONFLICT BACKSTORY

❑ REVIEWED?

14

Title:

AUTHOR:

SERIES/GENRE:

DATE STARTED

/ /

DATE FINISHED

/ /

EBOOK PAPER AUDIO

MY RATING

☆ ☆ ☆ ☆ ☆

GREAT: CHARACTERS PLOT SUSPENSE DRAMA HUMOR HEROINE HERO ORIGINALITY ANGST EMOTIONS DIALOGUE ACTION WIT BANTER SEX SCENES SETTING DETAIL CONFLICT BACKSTORY

❑ REVIEWED?

Title:

AUTHOR: ______________________________

SERIES/GENRE: ______________________________

DATE STARTED

DATE FINISHED

EBOOK PAPER AUDIO

MY RATING

❑ REVIEWED?

GREAT: CHARACTERS PLOT SUSPENSE DRAMA HUMOR HEROINE HERO ORIGINALITY ANGST EMOTIONS DIALOGUE ACTION WIT BANTER SEX SCENES SETTING DETAIL CONFLICT BACKSTORY

Title:

AUTHOR: ______________________________

SERIES/GENRE: ______________________________

DATE STARTED

DATE FINISHED

EBOOK PAPER AUDIO

MY RATING

❑ REVIEWED?

GREAT: CHARACTERS PLOT SUSPENSE DRAMA HUMOR HEROINE HERO ORIGINALITY ANGST EMOTIONS DIALOGUE ACTION WIT BANTER SEX SCENES SETTING DETAIL CONFLICT BACKSTORY

17

Title:

AUTHOR:

SERIES/GENRE:

DATE STARTED

/ /

DATE FINISHED

/ /

EBOOK PAPER AUDIO

MY RATING

☐ REVIEWED?

GREAT: CHARACTERS PLOT SUSPENSE DRAMA HUMOR HEROINE HERO ORIGINALITY ANGST EMOTIONS DIALOGUE ACTION WIT BANTER SEX SCENES SETTING DETAIL CONFLICT BACKSTORY

18

Title:

AUTHOR:

SERIES/GENRE:

DATE STARTED

/ /

DATE FINISHED

/ /

EBOOK PAPER AUDIO

MY RATING

☐ REVIEWED?

GREAT: CHARACTERS PLOT SUSPENSE DRAMA HUMOR HEROINE HERO ORIGINALITY ANGST EMOTIONS DIALOGUE ACTION WIT BANTER SEX SCENES SETTING DETAIL CONFLICT BACKSTORY

Title:

AUTHOR:

SERIES/GENRE:

DATE STARTED

DATE FINISHED

EBOOK PAPER AUDIO

MY RATING

❑ REVIEWED?

GREAT: CHARACTERS PLOT SUSPENSE DRAMA HUMOR HEROINE HERO ORIGINALITY ANGST EMOTIONS DIALOGUE ACTION WIT BANTER SEX SCENES SETTING DETAIL CONFLICT BACKSTORY

Title:

AUTHOR:

SERIES/GENRE:

DATE STARTED

DATE FINISHED

EBOOK PAPER AUDIO

MY RATING

❑ REVIEWED?

GREAT: CHARACTERS PLOT SUSPENSE DRAMA HUMOR HEROINE HERO ORIGINALITY ANGST EMOTIONS DIALOGUE ACTION WIT BANTER SEX SCENES SETTING DETAIL CONFLICT BACKSTORY

Title:

AUTHOR: ______

DATE STARTED

/ /

SERIES/GENRE: ______

DATE FINISHED

/ /

EBOOK PAPER AUDIO

MY RATING

GREAT: CHARACTERS PLOT SUSPENSE DRAMA HUMOR HEROINE HERO ORIGINALITY ANGST EMOTIONS DIALOGUE ACTION WIT BANTER SEX SCENES SETTING DETAIL CONFLICT BACKSTORY

❏ REVIEWED?

22

Title:

AUTHOR: ______

DATE STARTED

/ /

SERIES/GENRE: ______

DATE FINISHED

/ /

EBOOK PAPER AUDIO

MY RATING

GREAT: CHARACTERS PLOT SUSPENSE DRAMA HUMOR HEROINE HERO ORIGINALITY ANGST EMOTIONS DIALOGUE ACTION WIT BANTER SEX SCENES SETTING DETAIL CONFLICT BACKSTORY

❏ REVIEWED?

23

Title:

AUTHOR:

SERIES/GENRE:

DATE STARTED

DATE FINISHED

EBOOK PAPER AUDIO

MY RATING

❑ REVIEWED?

GREAT: CHARACTERS PLOT SUSPENSE DRAMA HUMOR HEROINE HERO
ORIGINALITY ANGST EMOTIONS DIALOGUE ACTION WIT BANTER SEX SCENES
SETTING DETAIL CONFLICT BACKSTORY

Title:

AUTHOR:

SERIES/GENRE:

DATE STARTED

DATE FINISHED

EBOOK PAPER AUDIO

MY RATING

❑ REVIEWED?

GREAT: CHARACTERS PLOT SUSPENSE DRAMA HUMOR HEROINE HERO
ORIGINALITY ANGST EMOTIONS DIALOGUE ACTION WIT BANTER SEX SCENES
SETTING DETAIL CONFLICT BACKSTORY

Title:

AUTHOR:

SERIES/GENRE:

DATE STARTED

DATE FINISHED

EBOOK PAPER AUDIO

MY RATING

☆ ☆ ☆ ☆ ☆

❑ REVIEWED?

GREAT: CHARACTERS PLOT SUSPENSE DRAMA HUMOR HEROINE HERO ORIGINALITY ANGST EMOTIONS DIALOGUE ACTION WIT BANTER SEX SCENES SETTING DETAIL CONFLICT BACKSTORY

Title:

AUTHOR:

SERIES/GENRE:

DATE STARTED

DATE FINISHED

EBOOK PAPER AUDIO

MY RATING

☆ ☆ ☆ ☆ ☆

❑ REVIEWED?

GREAT: CHARACTERS PLOT SUSPENSE DRAMA HUMOR HEROINE HERO ORIGINALITY ANGST EMOTIONS DIALOGUE ACTION WIT BANTER SEX SCENES SETTING DETAIL CONFLICT BACKSTORY

Title:

AUTHOR:

SERIES/GENRE:

DATE STARTED

DATE FINISHED

EBOOK PAPER AUDIO

MY RATING

❑ REVIEWED?

GREAT: CHARACTERS PLOT SUSPENSE DRAMA HUMOR HEROINE HERO ORIGINALITY ANGST EMOTIONS DIALOGUE ACTION WIT BANTER SEX SCENES SETTING DETAIL CONFLICT BACKSTORY

Title:

AUTHOR:

SERIES/GENRE:

DATE STARTED

DATE FINISHED

EBOOK PAPER AUDIO

MY RATING

❑ REVIEWED?

GREAT: CHARACTERS PLOT SUSPENSE DRAMA HUMOR HEROINE HERO ORIGINALITY ANGST EMOTIONS DIALOGUE ACTION WIT BANTER SEX SCENES SETTING DETAIL CONFLICT BACKSTORY

29

Title:

AUTHOR:

SERIES/GENRE:

DATE STARTED

DATE FINISHED

EBOOK PAPER AUDIO

MY RATING

GREAT: CHARACTERS PLOT SUSPENSE DRAMA HUMOR HEROINE HERO ORIGINALITY ANGST EMOTIONS DIALOGUE ACTION WIT BANTER SEX SCENES SETTING DETAIL CONFLICT BACKSTORY

❑ REVIEWED?

30

Title:

AUTHOR:

SERIES/GENRE:

DATE STARTED

DATE FINISHED

EBOOK PAPER AUDIO

MY RATING

GREAT: CHARACTERS PLOT SUSPENSE DRAMA HUMOR HEROINE HERO ORIGINALITY ANGST EMOTIONS DIALOGUE ACTION WIT BANTER SEX SCENES SETTING DETAIL CONFLICT BACKSTORY

❑ REVIEWED?

Title:

AUTHOR: ______

DATE STARTED

SERIES/GENRE: ______

DATE FINISHED

EBOOK PAPER AUDIO

MY RATING

GREAT: CHARACTERS PLOT SUSPENSE DRAMA HUMOR HEROINE HERO ORIGINALITY ANGST EMOTIONS DIALOGUE ACTION WIT BANTER SEX SCENES SETTING DETAIL CONFLICT BACKSTORY

❏ REVIEWED?

Title:

AUTHOR: ______

DATE STARTED

SERIES/GENRE: ______

DATE FINISHED

EBOOK PAPER AUDIO

MY RATING

GREAT: CHARACTERS PLOT SUSPENSE DRAMA HUMOR HEROINE HERO ORIGINALITY ANGST EMOTIONS DIALOGUE ACTION WIT BANTER SEX SCENES SETTING DETAIL CONFLICT BACKSTORY

❏ REVIEWED?

Title:

AUTHOR:

SERIES/GENRE:

DATE STARTED

DATE FINISHED

EBOOK PAPER AUDIO

MY RATING

❑ REVIEWED?

GREAT: CHARACTERS PLOT SUSPENSE DRAMA HUMOR HEROINE HERO ORIGINALITY ANGST EMOTIONS DIALOGUE ACTION WIT BANTER SEX SCENES SETTING DETAIL CONFLICT BACKSTORY

Title:

AUTHOR:

SERIES/GENRE:

DATE STARTED

DATE FINISHED

EBOOK PAPER AUDIO

MY RATING

❑ REVIEWED?

GREAT: CHARACTERS PLOT SUSPENSE DRAMA HUMOR HEROINE HERO ORIGINALITY ANGST EMOTIONS DIALOGUE ACTION WIT BANTER SEX SCENES SETTING DETAIL CONFLICT BACKSTORY

Title:

AUTHOR:

SERIES/GENRE:

DATE STARTED

DATE FINISHED

EBOOK PAPER AUDIO

MY RATING

❑ REVIEWED?

GREAT: CHARACTERS PLOT SUSPENSE DRAMA HUMOR HEROINE HERO ORIGINALITY ANGST EMOTIONS DIALOGUE ACTION WIT BANTER SEX SCENES SETTING DETAIL CONFLICT BACKSTORY

Title:

AUTHOR:

SERIES/GENRE:

DATE STARTED

DATE FINISHED

EBOOK PAPER AUDIO

MY RATING

❑ REVIEWED?

GREAT: CHARACTERS PLOT SUSPENSE DRAMA HUMOR HEROINE HERO ORIGINALITY ANGST EMOTIONS DIALOGUE ACTION WIT BANTER SEX SCENES SETTING DETAIL CONFLICT BACKSTORY

Title:

AUTHOR:

SERIES/GENRE:

DATE STARTED

DATE FINISHED

EBOOK PAPER AUDIO

MY RATING

GREAT: CHARACTERS PLOT SUSPENSE DRAMA HUMOR HEROINE HERO ORIGINALITY ANGST EMOTIONS DIALOGUE ACTION WIT BANTER SEX SCENES SETTING DETAIL CONFLICT BACKSTORY

❑ REVIEWED?

38

Title:

AUTHOR:

SERIES/GENRE:

DATE STARTED

DATE FINISHED

EBOOK PAPER AUDIO

MY RATING

GREAT: CHARACTERS PLOT SUSPENSE DRAMA HUMOR HEROINE HERO ORIGINALITY ANGST EMOTIONS DIALOGUE ACTION WIT BANTER SEX SCENES SETTING DETAIL CONFLICT BACKSTORY

❑ REVIEWED?

“Books are a uniquely portable magic.”

STEPHEN KING

Title:

AUTHOR:

SERIES/GENRE:

DATE STARTED

/ /

DATE FINISHED

/ /

EBOOK PAPER AUDIO

MY RATING

☆ ☆ ☆ ☆ ☆

❑ REVIEWED?

GREAT: CHARACTERS PLOT SUSPENSE DRAMA HUMOR HEROINE HERO ORIGINALITY ANGST EMOTIONS DIALOGUE ACTION WIT BANTER SEX SCENES SETTING DETAIL CONFLICT BACKSTORY

40

Title:

AUTHOR:

SERIES/GENRE:

DATE STARTED

/ /

DATE FINISHED

/ /

EBOOK PAPER AUDIO

MY RATING

☆ ☆ ☆ ☆ ☆

❑ REVIEWED?

GREAT: CHARACTERS PLOT SUSPENSE DRAMA HUMOR HEROINE HERO ORIGINALITY ANGST EMOTIONS DIALOGUE ACTION WIT BANTER SEX SCENES SETTING DETAIL CONFLICT BACKSTORY

Title:

AUTHOR:

SERIES/GENRE:

DATE STARTED

DATE FINISHED

EBOOK PAPER AUDIO

MY RATING

☐ REVIEWED?

GREAT: CHARACTERS PLOT SUSPENSE DRAMA HUMOR HEROINE HERO ORIGINALITY ANGST EMOTIONS DIALOGUE ACTION WIT BANTER SEX SCENES SETTING DETAIL CONFLICT BACKSTORY

Title:

AUTHOR:

SERIES/GENRE:

DATE STARTED

DATE FINISHED

EBOOK PAPER AUDIO

MY RATING

☐ REVIEWED?

GREAT: CHARACTERS PLOT SUSPENSE DRAMA HUMOR HEROINE HERO ORIGINALITY ANGST EMOTIONS DIALOGUE ACTION WIT BANTER SEX SCENES SETTING DETAIL CONFLICT BACKSTORY

Title:

AUTHOR:

SERIES/GENRE:

DATE STARTED

DATE FINISHED

EBOOK PAPER AUDIO

MY RATING

GREAT: CHARACTERS PLOT SUSPENSE DRAMA HUMOR HEROINE HERO ORIGINALITY ANGST EMOTIONS DIALOGUE ACTION WIT BANTER SEX SCENES SETTING DETAIL CONFLICT BACKSTORY

❑ REVIEWED?

44

Title:

AUTHOR:

SERIES/GENRE:

DATE STARTED

DATE FINISHED

EBOOK PAPER AUDIO

MY RATING

GREAT: CHARACTERS PLOT SUSPENSE DRAMA HUMOR HEROINE HERO ORIGINALITY ANGST EMOTIONS DIALOGUE ACTION WIT BANTER SEX SCENES SETTING DETAIL CONFLICT BACKSTORY

❑ REVIEWED?

Title:

AUTHOR:

SERIES/GENRE:

DATE STARTED

DATE FINISHED

EBOOK PAPER AUDIO

MY RATING

❑ REVIEWED?

GREAT: CHARACTERS PLOT SUSPENSE DRAMA HUMOR HEROINE HERO ORIGINALITY ANGST EMOTIONS DIALOGUE ACTION WIT BANTER SEX SCENES SETTING DETAIL CONFLICT BACKSTORY

Title:

AUTHOR:

SERIES/GENRE:

DATE STARTED

DATE FINISHED

EBOOK PAPER AUDIO

MY RATING

❑ REVIEWED?

GREAT: CHARACTERS PLOT SUSPENSE DRAMA HUMOR HEROINE HERO ORIGINALITY ANGST EMOTIONS DIALOGUE ACTION WIT BANTER SEX SCENES SETTING DETAIL CONFLICT BACKSTORY

Title:

AUTHOR:

SERIES/GENRE:

DATE STARTED

DATE FINISHED

EBOOK PAPER AUDIO

MY RATING

❑ REVIEWED?

GREAT: CHARACTERS PLOT SUSPENSE DRAMA HUMOR HEROINE HERO ORIGINALITY ANGST EMOTIONS DIALOGUE ACTION WIT BANTER SEX SCENES SETTING DETAIL CONFLICT BACKSTORY

48

Title:

AUTHOR:

SERIES/GENRE:

DATE STARTED

DATE FINISHED

EBOOK PAPER AUDIO

MY RATING

❑ REVIEWED?

GREAT: CHARACTERS PLOT SUSPENSE DRAMA HUMOR HEROINE HERO ORIGINALITY ANGST EMOTIONS DIALOGUE ACTION WIT BANTER SEX SCENES SETTING DETAIL CONFLICT BACKSTORY

Title:

AUTHOR: ____________________

SERIES/GENRE: ____________________

DATE STARTED

DATE FINISHED

EBOOK PAPER AUDIO

MY RATING

☐ REVIEWED?

GREAT: CHARACTERS PLOT SUSPENSE DRAMA HUMOR HEROINE HERO ORIGINALITY ANGST EMOTIONS DIALOGUE ACTION WIT BANTER SEX SCENES SETTING DETAIL CONFLICT BACKSTORY

Title:

AUTHOR: ____________________

SERIES/GENRE: ____________________

DATE STARTED

DATE FINISHED

EBOOK PAPER AUDIO

MY RATING

☐ REVIEWED?

GREAT: CHARACTERS PLOT SUSPENSE DRAMA HUMOR HEROINE HERO ORIGINALITY ANGST EMOTIONS DIALOGUE ACTION WIT BANTER SEX SCENES SETTING DETAIL CONFLICT BACKSTORY

Title:

AUTHOR:

SERIES/GENRE:

DATE STARTED

DATE FINISHED

EBOOK PAPER AUDIO

MY RATING

❑ REVIEWED?

GREAT: CHARACTERS PLOT SUSPENSE DRAMA HUMOR HEROINE HERO ORIGINALITY ANGST EMOTIONS DIALOGUE ACTION WIT BANTER SEX SCENES SETTING DETAIL CONFLICT BACKSTORY

52

Title:

AUTHOR:

SERIES/GENRE:

DATE STARTED

DATE FINISHED

EBOOK PAPER AUDIO

MY RATING

❑ REVIEWED?

GREAT: CHARACTERS PLOT SUSPENSE DRAMA HUMOR HEROINE HERO ORIGINALITY ANGST EMOTIONS DIALOGUE ACTION WIT BANTER SEX SCENES SETTING DETAIL CONFLICT BACKSTORY

53

Title:

AUTHOR:

SERIES/GENRE:

DATE STARTED

DATE FINISHED

EBOOK PAPER AUDIO

MY RATING

☆ ☆ ☆ ☆ ☆

GREAT: CHARACTERS PLOT SUSPENSE DRAMA HUMOR HEROINE HERO ORIGINALITY ANGST EMOTIONS DIALOGUE ACTION WIT BANTER SEX SCENES SETTING DETAIL CONFLICT BACKSTORY

❑ REVIEWED?

Title:

AUTHOR:

SERIES/GENRE:

DATE STARTED

DATE FINISHED

EBOOK PAPER AUDIO

MY RATING

☆ ☆ ☆ ☆ ☆

GREAT: CHARACTERS PLOT SUSPENSE DRAMA HUMOR HEROINE HERO ORIGINALITY ANGST EMOTIONS DIALOGUE ACTION WIT BANTER SEX SCENES SETTING DETAIL CONFLICT BACKSTORY

❑ REVIEWED?

55

Title:

AUTHOR: ______

SERIES/GENRE: ______

DATE STARTED

/ /

DATE FINISHED

/ /

EBOOK PAPER AUDIO

MY RATING

☆ ☆ ☆ ☆ ☆

❑ REVIEWED?

GREAT: CHARACTERS PLOT SUSPENSE DRAMA HUMOR HEROINE HERO ORIGINALITY ANGST EMOTIONS DIALOGUE ACTION WIT BANTER SEX SCENES SETTING DETAIL CONFLICT BACKSTORY

56

Title:

AUTHOR: ______

SERIES/GENRE: ______

DATE STARTED

/ /

DATE FINISHED

/ /

EBOOK PAPER AUDIO

MY RATING

☆ ☆ ☆ ☆ ☆

❑ REVIEWED?

GREAT: CHARACTERS PLOT SUSPENSE DRAMA HUMOR HEROINE HERO ORIGINALITY ANGST EMOTIONS DIALOGUE ACTION WIT BANTER SEX SCENES SETTING DETAIL CONFLICT BACKSTORY

Title:

AUTHOR:

SERIES/GENRE:

DATE STARTED

DATE FINISHED

EBOOK PAPER AUDIO

MY RATING

❑ REVIEWED?

GREAT: CHARACTERS PLOT SUSPENSE DRAMA HUMOR HEROINE HERO ORIGINALITY ANGST EMOTIONS DIALOGUE ACTION WIT BANTER SEX SCENES SETTING DETAIL CONFLICT BACKSTORY

Title:

AUTHOR:

SERIES/GENRE:

DATE STARTED

DATE FINISHED

EBOOK PAPER AUDIO

MY RATING

❑ REVIEWED?

GREAT: CHARACTERS PLOT SUSPENSE DRAMA HUMOR HEROINE HERO ORIGINALITY ANGST EMOTIONS DIALOGUE ACTION WIT BANTER SEX SCENES SETTING DETAIL CONFLICT BACKSTORY

59

Title:

AUTHOR: ______

SERIES/GENRE: ______

DATE STARTED

/ /

DATE FINISHED

/ /

EBOOK PAPER AUDIO

MY RATING

☆ ☆ ☆ ☆ ☆

❑ REVIEWED?

GREAT: CHARACTERS PLOT SUSPENSE DRAMA HUMOR HEROINE HERO ORIGINALITY ANGST EMOTIONS DIALOGUE ACTION WIT BANTER SEX SCENES SETTING DETAIL CONFLICT BACKSTORY

60

Title:

AUTHOR: ______

SERIES/GENRE: ______

DATE STARTED

/ /

DATE FINISHED

/ /

EBOOK PAPER AUDIO

MY RATING

☆ ☆ ☆ ☆ ☆

❑ REVIEWED?

GREAT: CHARACTERS PLOT SUSPENSE DRAMA HUMOR HEROINE HERO ORIGINALITY ANGST EMOTIONS DIALOGUE ACTION WIT BANTER SEX SCENES SETTING DETAIL CONFLICT BACKSTORY

61

Title:

AUTHOR:

SERIES/GENRE:

DATE STARTED

DATE FINISHED

EBOOK PAPER AUDIO

MY RATING

GREAT: CHARACTERS PLOT SUSPENSE DRAMA HUMOR HEROINE HERO ORIGINALITY ANGST EMOTIONS DIALOGUE ACTION WIT BANTER SEX SCENES SETTING DETAIL CONFLICT BACKSTORY

❑ REVIEWED?

Title:

AUTHOR:

SERIES/GENRE:

DATE STARTED

DATE FINISHED

EBOOK PAPER AUDIO

MY RATING

GREAT: CHARACTERS PLOT SUSPENSE DRAMA HUMOR HEROINE HERO ORIGINALITY ANGST EMOTIONS DIALOGUE ACTION WIT BANTER SEX SCENES SETTING DETAIL CONFLICT BACKSTORY

❑ REVIEWED?

63

Title:

AUTHOR:

SERIES/GENRE:

DATE STARTED

/ /

DATE FINISHED

/ /

EBOOK PAPER AUDIO

MY RATING

☆ ☆ ☆ ☆ ☆

❑ REVIEWED?

GREAT: CHARACTERS PLOT SUSPENSE DRAMA HUMOR HEROINE HERO ORIGINALITY ANGST EMOTIONS DIALOGUE ACTION WIT BANTER SEX SCENES SETTING DETAIL CONFLICT BACKSTORY

64

Title:

AUTHOR:

SERIES/GENRE:

DATE STARTED

/ /

DATE FINISHED

/ /

EBOOK PAPER AUDIO

MY RATING

☆ ☆ ☆ ☆ ☆

❑ REVIEWED?

GREAT: CHARACTERS PLOT SUSPENSE DRAMA HUMOR HEROINE HERO ORIGINALITY ANGST EMOTIONS DIALOGUE ACTION WIT BANTER SEX SCENES SETTING DETAIL CONFLICT BACKSTORY

65

Title:

AUTHOR:

SERIES/GENRE:

DATE STARTED

DATE FINISHED

EBOOK PAPER AUDIO

MY RATING

☆☆☆☆☆

GREAT: CHARACTERS PLOT SUSPENSE DRAMA HUMOR HEROINE HERO ORIGINALITY ANGST EMOTIONS DIALOGUE ACTION WIT BANTER SEX SCENES SETTING DETAIL CONFLICT BACKSTORY

❑ REVIEWED?

Title:

AUTHOR:

SERIES/GENRE:

DATE STARTED

DATE FINISHED

EBOOK PAPER AUDIO

MY RATING

☆☆☆☆☆

GREAT: CHARACTERS PLOT SUSPENSE DRAMA HUMOR HEROINE HERO ORIGINALITY ANGST EMOTIONS DIALOGUE ACTION WIT BANTER SEX SCENES SETTING DETAIL CONFLICT BACKSTORY

❑ REVIEWED?

Title:

AUTHOR:

SERIES/GENRE:

DATE STARTED

DATE FINISHED

EBOOK PAPER AUDIO

MY RATING

❏ REVIEWED?

GREAT: CHARACTERS PLOT SUSPENSE DRAMA HUMOR HEROINE HERO ORIGINALITY ANGST EMOTIONS DIALOGUE ACTION WIT BANTER SEX SCENES SETTING DETAIL CONFLICT BACKSTORY

Title:

AUTHOR:

SERIES/GENRE:

DATE STARTED

DATE FINISHED

EBOOK PAPER AUDIO

MY RATING

❏ REVIEWED?

GREAT: CHARACTERS PLOT SUSPENSE DRAMA HUMOR HEROINE HERO ORIGINALITY ANGST EMOTIONS DIALOGUE ACTION WIT BANTER SEX SCENES SETTING DETAIL CONFLICT BACKSTORY

Title:

AUTHOR:

SERIES/GENRE:

DATE STARTED

DATE FINISHED

EBOOK PAPER AUDIO

MY RATING

❏ REVIEWED?

GREAT: CHARACTERS PLOT SUSPENSE DRAMA HUMOR HEROINE HERO ORIGINALITY ANGST EMOTIONS DIALOGUE ACTION WIT BANTER SEX SCENES SETTING DETAIL CONFLICT BACKSTORY

Title:

AUTHOR:

SERIES/GENRE:

DATE STARTED

DATE FINISHED

EBOOK PAPER AUDIO

MY RATING

❏ REVIEWED?

GREAT: CHARACTERS PLOT SUSPENSE DRAMA HUMOR HEROINE HERO ORIGINALITY ANGST EMOTIONS DIALOGUE ACTION WIT BANTER SEX SCENES SETTING DETAIL CONFLICT BACKSTORY

71

Title:

AUTHOR:

SERIES/GENRE:

DATE STARTED

/ /

DATE FINISHED

/ /

EBOOK PAPER AUDIO

MY RATING

☆ ☆ ☆ ☆ ☆

❑ REVIEWED?

GREAT: CHARACTERS PLOT SUSPENSE DRAMA HUMOR HEROINE HERO ORIGINALITY ANGST EMOTIONS DIALOGUE ACTION WIT BANTER SEX SCENES SETTING DETAIL CONFLICT BACKSTORY

72

Title:

AUTHOR:

SERIES/GENRE:

DATE STARTED

/ /

DATE FINISHED

/ /

EBOOK PAPER AUDIO

MY RATING

☆ ☆ ☆ ☆ ☆

❑ REVIEWED?

GREAT: CHARACTERS PLOT SUSPENSE DRAMA HUMOR HEROINE HERO ORIGINALITY ANGST EMOTIONS DIALOGUE ACTION WIT BANTER SEX SCENES SETTING DETAIL CONFLICT BACKSTORY

73

Title:

AUTHOR: ______________________

SERIES/GENRE: ______________________

DATE STARTED

DATE FINISHED

EBOOK PAPER AUDIO

MY RATING

☆ ☆ ☆ ☆ ☆

❑ REVIEWED?

GREAT: CHARACTERS PLOT SUSPENSE DRAMA HUMOR HEROINE HERO ORIGINALITY ANGST EMOTIONS DIALOGUE ACTION WIT BANTER SEX SCENES SETTING DETAIL CONFLICT BACKSTORY

Title:

AUTHOR: ______________________

SERIES/GENRE: ______________________

DATE STARTED

DATE FINISHED

EBOOK PAPER AUDIO

MY RATING

☆ ☆ ☆ ☆ ☆

❑ REVIEWED?

GREAT: CHARACTERS PLOT SUSPENSE DRAMA HUMOR HEROINE HERO ORIGINALITY ANGST EMOTIONS DIALOGUE ACTION WIT BANTER SEX SCENES SETTING DETAIL CONFLICT BACKSTORY

Title:

AUTHOR:

SERIES/GENRE:

DATE STARTED

DATE FINISHED

EBOOK PAPER AUDIO

MY RATING

❑ REVIEWED?

GREAT: CHARACTERS PLOT SUSPENSE DRAMA HUMOR HEROINE HERO ORIGINALITY ANGST EMOTIONS DIALOGUE ACTION WIT BANTER SEX SCENES SETTING DETAIL CONFLICT BACKSTORY

76

Title:

AUTHOR:

SERIES/GENRE:

DATE STARTED

DATE FINISHED

EBOOK PAPER AUDIO

MY RATING

❑ REVIEWED?

GREAT: CHARACTERS PLOT SUSPENSE DRAMA HUMOR HEROINE HERO ORIGINALITY ANGST EMOTIONS DIALOGUE ACTION WIT BANTER SEX SCENES SETTING DETAIL CONFLICT BACKSTORY

Title:

AUTHOR:

DATE STARTED

SERIES/GENRE:

DATE FINISHED

EBOOK PAPER AUDIO

MY RATING

GREAT: CHARACTERS PLOT SUSPENSE DRAMA HUMOR HEROINE HERO ORIGINALITY ANGST EMOTIONS DIALOGUE ACTION WIT BANTER SEX SCENES SETTING DETAIL CONFLICT BACKSTORY

❑ REVIEWED?

Title:

AUTHOR:

DATE STARTED

SERIES/GENRE:

DATE FINISHED

EBOOK PAPER AUDIO

MY RATING

GREAT: CHARACTERS PLOT SUSPENSE DRAMA HUMOR HEROINE HERO ORIGINALITY ANGST EMOTIONS DIALOGUE ACTION WIT BANTER SEX SCENES SETTING DETAIL CONFLICT BACKSTORY

❑ REVIEWED?

“Where is human nature so weak as in the bookstore?”

HENRY WARD BEECHER

79

Title:

AUTHOR:

DATE STARTED

SERIES/GENRE:

DATE FINISHED

EBOOK PAPER AUDIO

MY RATING

GREAT: CHARACTERS PLOT SUSPENSE DRAMA HUMOR HEROINE HERO ORIGINALITY ANGST EMOTIONS DIALOGUE ACTION WIT BANTER SEX SCENES SETTING DETAIL CONFLICT BACKSTORY

❑ REVIEWED?

Title:

AUTHOR:

DATE STARTED

SERIES/GENRE:

DATE FINISHED

EBOOK PAPER AUDIO

MY RATING

GREAT: CHARACTERS PLOT SUSPENSE DRAMA HUMOR HEROINE HERO ORIGINALITY ANGST EMOTIONS DIALOGUE ACTION WIT BANTER SEX SCENES SETTING DETAIL CONFLICT BACKSTORY

❑ REVIEWED?

Title:

AUTHOR:

SERIES/GENRE:

DATE STARTED

DATE FINISHED

EBOOK PAPER AUDIO

MY RATING

❑ REVIEWED?

GREAT: CHARACTERS PLOT SUSPENSE DRAMA HUMOR HEROINE HERO ORIGINALITY ANGST EMOTIONS DIALOGUE ACTION WIT BANTER SEX SCENES SETTING DETAIL CONFLICT BACKSTORY

82

Title:

AUTHOR:

SERIES/GENRE:

DATE STARTED

DATE FINISHED

EBOOK PAPER AUDIO

MY RATING

❑ REVIEWED?

GREAT: CHARACTERS PLOT SUSPENSE DRAMA HUMOR HEROINE HERO ORIGINALITY ANGST EMOTIONS DIALOGUE ACTION WIT BANTER SEX SCENES SETTING DETAIL CONFLICT BACKSTORY

Title:

AUTHOR:

SERIES/GENRE:

DATE STARTED

DATE FINISHED

EBOOK PAPER AUDIO

MY RATING

☐ REVIEWED?

GREAT: CHARACTERS PLOT SUSPENSE DRAMA HUMOR HEROINE HERO ORIGINALITY ANGST EMOTIONS DIALOGUE ACTION WIT BANTER SEX SCENES SETTING DETAIL CONFLICT BACKSTORY

Title:

AUTHOR:

SERIES/GENRE:

DATE STARTED

DATE FINISHED

EBOOK PAPER AUDIO

MY RATING

☐ REVIEWED?

GREAT: CHARACTERS PLOT SUSPENSE DRAMA HUMOR HEROINE HERO ORIGINALITY ANGST EMOTIONS DIALOGUE ACTION WIT BANTER SEX SCENES SETTING DETAIL CONFLICT BACKSTORY

85

Title:

AUTHOR:

SERIES/GENRE:

DATE STARTED

DATE FINISHED

EBOOK PAPER AUDIO

MY RATING

❑ REVIEWED?

GREAT: CHARACTERS PLOT SUSPENSE DRAMA HUMOR HEROINE HERO ORIGINALITY ANGST EMOTIONS DIALOGUE ACTION WIT BANTER SEX SCENES SETTING DETAIL CONFLICT BACKSTORY

86

Title:

AUTHOR:

SERIES/GENRE:

DATE STARTED

DATE FINISHED

EBOOK PAPER AUDIO

MY RATING

❑ REVIEWED?

GREAT: CHARACTERS PLOT SUSPENSE DRAMA HUMOR HEROINE HERO ORIGINALITY ANGST EMOTIONS DIALOGUE ACTION WIT BANTER SEX SCENES SETTING DETAIL CONFLICT BACKSTORY

87

Title:

AUTHOR:

SERIES/GENRE:

DATE STARTED

DATE FINISHED

EBOOK PAPER AUDIO

MY RATING

☆ ☆ ☆ ☆ ☆

❑ REVIEWED?

GREAT: CHARACTERS PLOT SUSPENSE DRAMA HUMOR HEROINE HERO ORIGINALITY ANGST EMOTIONS DIALOGUE ACTION WIT BANTER SEX SCENES SETTING DETAIL CONFLICT BACKSTORY

88

Title:

AUTHOR:

SERIES/GENRE:

DATE STARTED

DATE FINISHED

EBOOK PAPER AUDIO

MY RATING

☆ ☆ ☆ ☆ ☆

❑ REVIEWED?

GREAT: CHARACTERS PLOT SUSPENSE DRAMA HUMOR HEROINE HERO ORIGINALITY ANGST EMOTIONS DIALOGUE ACTION WIT BANTER SEX SCENES SETTING DETAIL CONFLICT BACKSTORY

Title:

AUTHOR: ____________________

SERIES/GENRE: ____________________

DATE STARTED

/ /

DATE FINISHED

/ /

EBOOK PAPER AUDIO

MY RATING

☆ ☆ ☆ ☆ ☆

❑ REVIEWED?

GREAT: CHARACTERS PLOT SUSPENSE DRAMA HUMOR HEROINE HERO ORIGINALITY ANGST EMOTIONS DIALOGUE ACTION WIT BANTER SEX SCENES SETTING DETAIL CONFLICT BACKSTORY

Title:

AUTHOR: ____________________

SERIES/GENRE: ____________________

DATE STARTED

/ /

DATE FINISHED

/ /

EBOOK PAPER AUDIO

MY RATING

☆ ☆ ☆ ☆ ☆

❑ REVIEWED?

GREAT: CHARACTERS PLOT SUSPENSE DRAMA HUMOR HEROINE HERO ORIGINALITY ANGST EMOTIONS DIALOGUE ACTION WIT BANTER SEX SCENES SETTING DETAIL CONFLICT BACKSTORY

Title:

AUTHOR:

SERIES/GENRE:

DATE STARTED

/ /

DATE FINISHED

/ /

EBOOK PAPER AUDIO

MY RATING

GREAT: CHARACTERS PLOT SUSPENSE DRAMA HUMOR HEROINE HERO ORIGINALITY ANGST EMOTIONS DIALOGUE ACTION WIT BANTER SEX SCENES SETTING DETAIL CONFLICT BACKSTORY

❑ REVIEWED?

Title:

AUTHOR:

SERIES/GENRE:

DATE STARTED

/ /

DATE FINISHED

/ /

EBOOK PAPER AUDIO

MY RATING

GREAT: CHARACTERS PLOT SUSPENSE DRAMA HUMOR HEROINE HERO ORIGINALITY ANGST EMOTIONS DIALOGUE ACTION WIT BANTER SEX SCENES SETTING DETAIL CONFLICT BACKSTORY

❑ REVIEWED?

Title:

AUTHOR:

SERIES/GENRE:

DATE STARTED

DATE FINISHED

EBOOK PAPER AUDIO

MY RATING

❑ REVIEWED?

GREAT: CHARACTERS PLOT SUSPENSE DRAMA HUMOR HEROINE HERO ORIGINALITY ANGST EMOTIONS DIALOGUE ACTION WIT BANTER SEX SCENES SETTING DETAIL CONFLICT BACKSTORY

Title:

AUTHOR:

SERIES/GENRE:

DATE STARTED

DATE FINISHED

EBOOK PAPER AUDIO

MY RATING

❑ REVIEWED?

GREAT: CHARACTERS PLOT SUSPENSE DRAMA HUMOR HEROINE HERO ORIGINALITY ANGST EMOTIONS DIALOGUE ACTION WIT BANTER SEX SCENES SETTING DETAIL CONFLICT BACKSTORY

Title:

AUTHOR:

SERIES/GENRE:

DATE STARTED

DATE FINISHED

EBOOK PAPER AUDIO

MY RATING

❑ REVIEWED?

GREAT: CHARACTERS PLOT SUSPENSE DRAMA HUMOR HEROINE HERO ORIGINALITY ANGST EMOTIONS DIALOGUE ACTION WIT BANTER SEX SCENES SETTING DETAIL CONFLICT BACKSTORY

Title:

AUTHOR:

SERIES/GENRE:

DATE STARTED

DATE FINISHED

EBOOK PAPER AUDIO

MY RATING

❑ REVIEWED?

GREAT: CHARACTERS PLOT SUSPENSE DRAMA HUMOR HEROINE HERO ORIGINALITY ANGST EMOTIONS DIALOGUE ACTION WIT BANTER SEX SCENES SETTING DETAIL CONFLICT BACKSTORY

Title:

AUTHOR:

SERIES/GENRE:

DATE STARTED

DATE FINISHED

EBOOK PAPER AUDIO

MY RATING

❑ REVIEWED?

GREAT: CHARACTERS PLOT SUSPENSE DRAMA HUMOR HEROINE HERO ORIGINALITY ANGST EMOTIONS DIALOGUE ACTION WIT BANTER SEX SCENES SETTING DETAIL CONFLICT BACKSTORY

98

Title:

AUTHOR:

SERIES/GENRE:

DATE STARTED

DATE FINISHED

EBOOK PAPER AUDIO

MY RATING

❑ REVIEWED?

GREAT: CHARACTERS PLOT SUSPENSE DRAMA HUMOR HEROINE HERO ORIGINALITY ANGST EMOTIONS DIALOGUE ACTION WIT BANTER SEX SCENES SETTING DETAIL CONFLICT BACKSTORY

Title:

AUTHOR:

SERIES/GENRE:

DATE STARTED

/ /

DATE FINISHED

/ /

EBOOK PAPER AUDIO

MY RATING

☆ ☆ ☆ ☆ ☆

❏ REVIEWED?

GREAT: CHARACTERS PLOT SUSPENSE DRAMA HUMOR HEROINE HERO ORIGINALITY ANGST EMOTIONS DIALOGUE ACTION WIT BANTER SEX SCENES SETTING DETAIL CONFLICT BACKSTORY

100

Title:

AUTHOR:

SERIES/GENRE:

DATE STARTED

/ /

DATE FINISHED

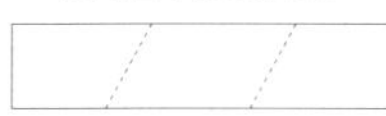

/ /

EBOOK PAPER AUDIO

MY RATING

❏ REVIEWED?

GREAT: CHARACTERS PLOT SUSPENSE DRAMA HUMOR HEROINE HERO ORIGINALITY ANGST EMOTIONS DIALOGUE ACTION WIT BANTER SEX SCENES SETTING DETAIL CONFLICT BACKSTORY

Title:

AUTHOR:

SERIES/GENRE:

DATE STARTED

DATE FINISHED

EBOOK PAPER AUDIO

MY RATING

❑ REVIEWED?

GREAT: CHARACTERS PLOT SUSPENSE DRAMA HUMOR HEROINE HERO ORIGINALITY ANGST EMOTIONS DIALOGUE ACTION WIT BANTER SEX SCENES SETTING DETAIL CONFLICT BACKSTORY

Title:

AUTHOR:

SERIES/GENRE:

DATE STARTED

DATE FINISHED

EBOOK PAPER AUDIO

MY RATING

❑ REVIEWED?

GREAT: CHARACTERS PLOT SUSPENSE DRAMA HUMOR HEROINE HERO ORIGINALITY ANGST EMOTIONS DIALOGUE ACTION WIT BANTER SEX SCENES SETTING DETAIL CONFLICT BACKSTORY

103

Title:

AUTHOR:

SERIES/GENRE:

DATE STARTED

DATE FINISHED

EBOOK PAPER AUDIO

MY RATING

❑ REVIEWED?

GREAT: CHARACTERS PLOT SUSPENSE DRAMA HUMOR HEROINE HERO ORIGINALITY ANGST EMOTIONS DIALOGUE ACTION WIT BANTER SEX SCENES SETTING DETAIL CONFLICT BACKSTORY

104

Title:

AUTHOR:

SERIES/GENRE:

DATE STARTED

DATE FINISHED

EBOOK PAPER AUDIO

MY RATING

❑ REVIEWED?

GREAT: CHARACTERS PLOT SUSPENSE DRAMA HUMOR HEROINE HERO ORIGINALITY ANGST EMOTIONS DIALOGUE ACTION WIT BANTER SEX SCENES SETTING DETAIL CONFLICT BACKSTORY

Title:

AUTHOR:

SERIES/GENRE:

DATE STARTED

DATE FINISHED

EBOOK PAPER AUDIO

MY RATING

❑ REVIEWED?

GREAT: CHARACTERS PLOT SUSPENSE DRAMA HUMOR HEROINE HERO ORIGINALITY ANGST EMOTIONS DIALOGUE ACTION WIT BANTER SEX SCENES SETTING DETAIL CONFLICT BACKSTORY

Title:

AUTHOR:

SERIES/GENRE:

DATE STARTED

DATE FINISHED

EBOOK PAPER AUDIO

MY RATING

❑ REVIEWED?

GREAT: CHARACTERS PLOT SUSPENSE DRAMA HUMOR HEROINE HERO ORIGINALITY ANGST EMOTIONS DIALOGUE ACTION WIT BANTER SEX SCENES SETTING DETAIL CONFLICT BACKSTORY

Title:

AUTHOR:

SERIES/GENRE:

DATE STARTED

DATE FINISHED

EBOOK PAPER AUDIO

MY RATING

❑ REVIEWED?

GREAT: CHARACTERS PLOT SUSPENSE DRAMA HUMOR HEROINE HERO ORIGINALITY ANGST EMOTIONS DIALOGUE ACTION WIT BANTER SEX SCENES SETTING DETAIL CONFLICT BACKSTORY

Title:

AUTHOR:

SERIES/GENRE:

DATE STARTED

DATE FINISHED

EBOOK PAPER AUDIO

MY RATING

❑ REVIEWED?

GREAT: CHARACTERS PLOT SUSPENSE DRAMA HUMOR HEROINE HERO ORIGINALITY ANGST EMOTIONS DIALOGUE ACTION WIT BANTER SEX SCENES SETTING DETAIL CONFLICT BACKSTORY

109

Title:

AUTHOR:

SERIES/GENRE:

DATE STARTED

/ /

DATE FINISHED

/ /

EBOOK PAPER AUDIO

MY RATING

❑ REVIEWED?

GREAT: CHARACTERS PLOT SUSPENSE DRAMA HUMOR HEROINE HERO ORIGINALITY ANGST EMOTIONS DIALOGUE ACTION WIT BANTER SEX SCENES SETTING DETAIL CONFLICT BACKSTORY

110

Title:

AUTHOR:

SERIES/GENRE:

DATE STARTED

/ /

DATE FINISHED

/ /

EBOOK PAPER AUDIO

MY RATING

❑ REVIEWED?

GREAT: CHARACTERS PLOT SUSPENSE DRAMA HUMOR HEROINE HERO ORIGINALITY ANGST EMOTIONS DIALOGUE ACTION WIT BANTER SEX SCENES SETTING DETAIL CONFLICT BACKSTORY

Title:

AUTHOR:

SERIES/GENRE:

DATE STARTED

DATE FINISHED

EBOOK PAPER AUDIO

MY RATING

❑ REVIEWED?

GREAT: CHARACTERS PLOT SUSPENSE DRAMA HUMOR HEROINE HERO ORIGINALITY ANGST EMOTIONS DIALOGUE ACTION WIT BANTER SEX SCENES SETTING DETAIL CONFLICT BACKSTORY

Title:

AUTHOR:

SERIES/GENRE:

DATE STARTED

DATE FINISHED

EBOOK PAPER AUDIO

MY RATING

❑ REVIEWED?

GREAT: CHARACTERS PLOT SUSPENSE DRAMA HUMOR HEROINE HERO ORIGINALITY ANGST EMOTIONS DIALOGUE ACTION WIT BANTER SEX SCENES SETTING DETAIL CONFLICT BACKSTORY

Title:

AUTHOR:

SERIES/GENRE:

DATE STARTED

/ /

DATE FINISHED

/ /

EBOOK PAPER AUDIO

MY RATING

❑ REVIEWED?

GREAT: CHARACTERS PLOT SUSPENSE DRAMA HUMOR HEROINE HERO ORIGINALITY ANGST EMOTIONS DIALOGUE ACTION WIT BANTER SEX SCENES SETTING DETAIL CONFLICT BACKSTORY

Title:

AUTHOR:

SERIES/GENRE:

DATE STARTED

/ /

DATE FINISHED

/ /

EBOOK PAPER AUDIO

MY RATING

❑ REVIEWED?

GREAT: CHARACTERS PLOT SUSPENSE DRAMA HUMOR HEROINE HERO ORIGINALITY ANGST EMOTIONS DIALOGUE ACTION WIT BANTER SEX SCENES SETTING DETAIL CONFLICT BACKSTORY

Title:

AUTHOR:

DATE STARTED

SERIES/GENRE:

DATE FINISHED

EBOOK PAPER AUDIO

MY RATING

GREAT: CHARACTERS PLOT SUSPENSE DRAMA HUMOR HEROINE HERO ORIGINALITY ANGST EMOTIONS DIALOGUE ACTION WIT BANTER SEX SCENES SETTING DETAIL CONFLICT BACKSTORY

❑ REVIEWED?

Title:

AUTHOR:

DATE STARTED

SERIES/GENRE:

DATE FINISHED

EBOOK PAPER AUDIO

MY RATING

GREAT: CHARACTERS PLOT SUSPENSE DRAMA HUMOR HEROINE HERO ORIGINALITY ANGST EMOTIONS DIALOGUE ACTION WIT BANTER SEX SCENES SETTING DETAIL CONFLICT BACKSTORY

❑ REVIEWED?

Title:

AUTHOR:

DATE STARTED

SERIES/GENRE:

DATE FINISHED

EBOOK PAPER AUDIO

MY RATING

GREAT: CHARACTERS PLOT SUSPENSE DRAMA HUMOR HEROINE HERO ORIGINALITY ANGST EMOTIONS DIALOGUE ACTION WIT BANTER SEX SCENES SETTING DETAIL CONFLICT BACKSTORY

❑ REVIEWED?

Title:

AUTHOR:

DATE STARTED

SERIES/GENRE:

DATE FINISHED

EBOOK PAPER AUDIO

MY RATING

GREAT: CHARACTERS PLOT SUSPENSE DRAMA HUMOR HEROINE HERO ORIGINALITY ANGST EMOTIONS DIALOGUE ACTION WIT BANTER SEX SCENES SETTING DETAIL CONFLICT BACKSTORY

❑ REVIEWED?

"The world was hers for the reading."

BETTY SMITH

Title:

AUTHOR:

DATE STARTED

SERIES/GENRE:

DATE FINISHED

EBOOK PAPER AUDIO

MY RATING

GREAT: CHARACTERS PLOT SUSPENSE DRAMA HUMOR HEROINE HERO ORIGINALITY ANGST EMOTIONS DIALOGUE ACTION WIT BANTER SEX SCENES SETTING DETAIL CONFLICT BACKSTORY

❑ REVIEWED?

Title:

AUTHOR:

DATE STARTED

SERIES/GENRE:

DATE FINISHED

EBOOK PAPER AUDIO

MY RATING

GREAT: CHARACTERS PLOT SUSPENSE DRAMA HUMOR HEROINE HERO ORIGINALITY ANGST EMOTIONS DIALOGUE ACTION WIT BANTER SEX SCENES SETTING DETAIL CONFLICT BACKSTORY

❑ REVIEWED?

Title:

AUTHOR:

SERIES/GENRE:

DATE STARTED

DATE FINISHED

EBOOK PAPER AUDIO

MY RATING

☐ REVIEWED?

GREAT: CHARACTERS PLOT SUSPENSE DRAMA HUMOR HEROINE HERO ORIGINALITY ANGST EMOTIONS DIALOGUE ACTION WIT BANTER SEX SCENES SETTING DETAIL CONFLICT BACKSTORY

Title:

AUTHOR:

SERIES/GENRE:

DATE STARTED

DATE FINISHED

EBOOK PAPER AUDIO

MY RATING

☐ REVIEWED?

GREAT: CHARACTERS PLOT SUSPENSE DRAMA HUMOR HEROINE HERO ORIGINALITY ANGST EMOTIONS DIALOGUE ACTION WIT BANTER SEX SCENES SETTING DETAIL CONFLICT BACKSTORY

Title:

AUTHOR:

SERIES/GENRE:

DATE STARTED

DATE FINISHED

EBOOK PAPER AUDIO

MY RATING

GREAT: CHARACTERS PLOT SUSPENSE DRAMA HUMOR HEROINE HERO ORIGINALITY ANGST EMOTIONS DIALOGUE ACTION WIT BANTER SEX SCENES SETTING DETAIL CONFLICT BACKSTORY

❑ REVIEWED?

Title:

AUTHOR:

SERIES/GENRE:

DATE STARTED

DATE FINISHED

EBOOK PAPER AUDIO

MY RATING

GREAT: CHARACTERS PLOT SUSPENSE DRAMA HUMOR HEROINE HERO ORIGINALITY ANGST EMOTIONS DIALOGUE ACTION WIT BANTER SEX SCENES SETTING DETAIL CONFLICT BACKSTORY

❑ REVIEWED?

125

Title:

AUTHOR:

SERIES/GENRE:

DATE STARTED

DATE FINISHED

EBOOK PAPER AUDIO

MY RATING

❑ REVIEWED?

GREAT: CHARACTERS PLOT SUSPENSE DRAMA HUMOR HEROINE HERO ORIGINALITY ANGST EMOTIONS DIALOGUE ACTION WIT BANTER SEX SCENES SETTING DETAIL CONFLICT BACKSTORY

126

Title:

AUTHOR:

SERIES/GENRE:

DATE STARTED

DATE FINISHED

EBOOK PAPER AUDIO

MY RATING

❑ REVIEWED?

GREAT: CHARACTERS PLOT SUSPENSE DRAMA HUMOR HEROINE HERO ORIGINALITY ANGST EMOTIONS DIALOGUE ACTION WIT BANTER SEX SCENES SETTING DETAIL CONFLICT BACKSTORY

Title:

AUTHOR:

DATE STARTED

SERIES/GENRE:

DATE FINISHED

EBOOK PAPER AUDIO

MY RATING

GREAT: CHARACTERS PLOT SUSPENSE DRAMA HUMOR HEROINE HERO ORIGINALITY ANGST EMOTIONS DIALOGUE ACTION WIT BANTER SEX SCENES SETTING DETAIL CONFLICT BACKSTORY

❑ REVIEWED?

Title:

AUTHOR:

DATE STARTED

SERIES/GENRE:

DATE FINISHED

EBOOK PAPER AUDIO

MY RATING

GREAT: CHARACTERS PLOT SUSPENSE DRAMA HUMOR HEROINE HERO ORIGINALITY ANGST EMOTIONS DIALOGUE ACTION WIT BANTER SEX SCENES SETTING DETAIL CONFLICT BACKSTORY

❑ REVIEWED?

Title:

AUTHOR:

DATE STARTED

SERIES/GENRE:

DATE FINISHED

EBOOK PAPER AUDIO

MY RATING

GREAT: CHARACTERS PLOT SUSPENSE DRAMA HUMOR HEROINE HERO ORIGINALITY ANGST EMOTIONS DIALOGUE ACTION WIT BANTER SEX SCENES SETTING DETAIL CONFLICT BACKSTORY

❑ REVIEWED?

Title:

AUTHOR:

DATE STARTED

SERIES/GENRE:

DATE FINISHED

EBOOK PAPER AUDIO

MY RATING

GREAT: CHARACTERS PLOT SUSPENSE DRAMA HUMOR HEROINE HERO ORIGINALITY ANGST EMOTIONS DIALOGUE ACTION WIT BANTER SEX SCENES SETTING DETAIL CONFLICT BACKSTORY

❑ REVIEWED?

131

Title:

AUTHOR:

SERIES/GENRE:

DATE STARTED

DATE FINISHED

EBOOK PAPER AUDIO

MY RATING

☆ ☆ ☆ ☆ ☆

❑ REVIEWED?

GREAT: CHARACTERS PLOT SUSPENSE DRAMA HUMOR HEROINE HERO ORIGINALITY ANGST EMOTIONS DIALOGUE ACTION WIT BANTER SEX SCENES SETTING DETAIL CONFLICT BACKSTORY

132

Title:

AUTHOR:

SERIES/GENRE:

DATE STARTED

DATE FINISHED

EBOOK PAPER AUDIO

MY RATING

☆ ☆ ☆ ☆ ☆

❑ REVIEWED?

GREAT: CHARACTERS PLOT SUSPENSE DRAMA HUMOR HEROINE HERO ORIGINALITY ANGST EMOTIONS DIALOGUE ACTION WIT BANTER SEX SCENES SETTING DETAIL CONFLICT BACKSTORY

Title:

AUTHOR:

SERIES/GENRE:

DATE STARTED

DATE FINISHED

EBOOK PAPER AUDIO

MY RATING

❑ REVIEWED?

GREAT: CHARACTERS PLOT SUSPENSE DRAMA HUMOR HEROINE HERO ORIGINALITY ANGST EMOTIONS DIALOGUE ACTION WIT BANTER SEX SCENES SETTING DETAIL CONFLICT BACKSTORY

134

Title:

AUTHOR:

SERIES/GENRE:

DATE STARTED

DATE FINISHED

EBOOK PAPER AUDIO

MY RATING

❑ REVIEWED?

GREAT: CHARACTERS PLOT SUSPENSE DRAMA HUMOR HEROINE HERO ORIGINALITY ANGST EMOTIONS DIALOGUE ACTION WIT BANTER SEX SCENES SETTING DETAIL CONFLICT BACKSTORY

Title:

AUTHOR:

SERIES/GENRE:

DATE STARTED

DATE FINISHED

EBOOK PAPER AUDIO

MY RATING

❏ REVIEWED?

GREAT: CHARACTERS PLOT SUSPENSE DRAMA HUMOR HEROINE HERO ORIGINALITY ANGST EMOTIONS DIALOGUE ACTION WIT BANTER SEX SCENES SETTING DETAIL CONFLICT BACKSTORY

Title:

AUTHOR:

SERIES/GENRE:

DATE STARTED

DATE FINISHED

EBOOK PAPER AUDIO

MY RATING

❏ REVIEWED?

GREAT: CHARACTERS PLOT SUSPENSE DRAMA HUMOR HEROINE HERO ORIGINALITY ANGST EMOTIONS DIALOGUE ACTION WIT BANTER SEX SCENES SETTING DETAIL CONFLICT BACKSTORY

Title:

AUTHOR:

SERIES/GENRE:

DATE STARTED

DATE FINISHED

EBOOK PAPER AUDIO

MY RATING

☐ REVIEWED?

GREAT: CHARACTERS PLOT SUSPENSE DRAMA HUMOR HEROINE HERO ORIGINALITY ANGST EMOTIONS DIALOGUE ACTION WIT BANTER SEX SCENES SETTING DETAIL CONFLICT BACKSTORY

Title:

AUTHOR:

SERIES/GENRE:

DATE STARTED

DATE FINISHED

EBOOK PAPER AUDIO

MY RATING

☐ REVIEWED?

GREAT: CHARACTERS PLOT SUSPENSE DRAMA HUMOR HEROINE HERO ORIGINALITY ANGST EMOTIONS DIALOGUE ACTION WIT BANTER SEX SCENES SETTING DETAIL CONFLICT BACKSTORY

139

Title:

AUTHOR:

DATE STARTED

SERIES/GENRE:

DATE FINISHED

EBOOK PAPER AUDIO

MY RATING

GREAT: CHARACTERS PLOT SUSPENSE DRAMA HUMOR HEROINE HERO ORIGINALITY ANGST EMOTIONS DIALOGUE ACTION WIT BANTER SEX SCENES SETTING DETAIL CONFLICT BACKSTORY

❑ REVIEWED?

140

Title:

AUTHOR:

DATE STARTED

SERIES/GENRE:

DATE FINISHED

EBOOK PAPER AUDIO

MY RATING

GREAT: CHARACTERS PLOT SUSPENSE DRAMA HUMOR HEROINE HERO ORIGINALITY ANGST EMOTIONS DIALOGUE ACTION WIT BANTER SEX SCENES SETTING DETAIL CONFLICT BACKSTORY

❑ REVIEWED?

Title:

AUTHOR:

SERIES/GENRE:

DATE STARTED

DATE FINISHED

EBOOK PAPER AUDIO

MY RATING

GREAT: CHARACTERS PLOT SUSPENSE DRAMA HUMOR HEROINE HERO ORIGINALITY ANGST EMOTIONS DIALOGUE ACTION WIT BANTER SEX SCENES SETTING DETAIL CONFLICT BACKSTORY

❑ REVIEWED?

Title:

AUTHOR:

SERIES/GENRE:

DATE STARTED

DATE FINISHED

EBOOK PAPER AUDIO

MY RATING

GREAT: CHARACTERS PLOT SUSPENSE DRAMA HUMOR HEROINE HERO ORIGINALITY ANGST EMOTIONS DIALOGUE ACTION WIT BANTER SEX SCENES SETTING DETAIL CONFLICT BACKSTORY

❑ REVIEWED?

Title:

AUTHOR:

SERIES/GENRE:

DATE STARTED

/ /

DATE FINISHED

/ /

EBOOK PAPER AUDIO

MY RATING

☆☆☆☆☆

GREAT: CHARACTERS PLOT SUSPENSE DRAMA HUMOR HEROINE HERO ORIGINALITY ANGST EMOTIONS DIALOGUE ACTION WIT BANTER SEX SCENES SETTING DETAIL CONFLICT BACKSTORY

❑ REVIEWED?

Title:

AUTHOR:

SERIES/GENRE:

DATE STARTED

/ /

DATE FINISHED

/ /

EBOOK PAPER AUDIO

MY RATING

☆☆☆☆☆

GREAT: CHARACTERS PLOT SUSPENSE DRAMA HUMOR HEROINE HERO ORIGINALITY ANGST EMOTIONS DIALOGUE ACTION WIT BANTER SEX SCENES SETTING DETAIL CONFLICT BACKSTORY

❑ REVIEWED?

Title:

AUTHOR:

SERIES/GENRE:

DATE STARTED

DATE FINISHED

EBOOK PAPER AUDIO

MY RATING

❑ REVIEWED?

GREAT: CHARACTERS PLOT SUSPENSE DRAMA HUMOR HEROINE HERO ORIGINALITY ANGST EMOTIONS DIALOGUE ACTION WIT BANTER SEX SCENES SETTING DETAIL CONFLICT BACKSTORY

Title:

AUTHOR:

SERIES/GENRE:

DATE STARTED

DATE FINISHED

EBOOK PAPER AUDIO

MY RATING

❑ REVIEWED?

GREAT: CHARACTERS PLOT SUSPENSE DRAMA HUMOR HEROINE HERO ORIGINALITY ANGST EMOTIONS DIALOGUE ACTION WIT BANTER SEX SCENES SETTING DETAIL CONFLICT BACKSTORY

Title:

AUTHOR:

SERIES/GENRE:

DATE STARTED

/ /

DATE FINISHED

/ /

EBOOK PAPER AUDIO

MY RATING

❑ REVIEWED?

GREAT: CHARACTERS PLOT SUSPENSE DRAMA HUMOR HEROINE HERO ORIGINALITY ANGST EMOTIONS DIALOGUE ACTION WIT BANTER SEX SCENES SETTING DETAIL CONFLICT BACKSTORY

Title:

AUTHOR:

SERIES/GENRE:

DATE STARTED

/ /

DATE FINISHED

/ /

EBOOK PAPER AUDIO

MY RATING

❑ REVIEWED?

GREAT: CHARACTERS PLOT SUSPENSE DRAMA HUMOR HEROINE HERO ORIGINALITY ANGST EMOTIONS DIALOGUE ACTION WIT BANTER SEX SCENES SETTING DETAIL CONFLICT BACKSTORY

Title:

AUTHOR:

SERIES/GENRE:

DATE STARTED

DATE FINISHED

EBOOK PAPER AUDIO

MY RATING

GREAT: CHARACTERS PLOT SUSPENSE DRAMA HUMOR HEROINE HERO ORIGINALITY ANGST EMOTIONS DIALOGUE ACTION WIT BANTER SEX SCENES SETTING DETAIL CONFLICT BACKSTORY

❑ REVIEWED?

Title:

AUTHOR:

SERIES/GENRE:

DATE STARTED

DATE FINISHED

EBOOK PAPER AUDIO

MY RATING

GREAT: CHARACTERS PLOT SUSPENSE DRAMA HUMOR HEROINE HERO ORIGINALITY ANGST EMOTIONS DIALOGUE ACTION WIT BANTER SEX SCENES SETTING DETAIL CONFLICT BACKSTORY

❑ REVIEWED?

Title:

AUTHOR:

DATE STARTED

SERIES/GENRE:

DATE FINISHED

T

EBOOK PAPER AUDIO

MY RATING

GREAT: CHARACTERS PLOT SUSPENSE DRAMA HUMOR HEROINE HERO
ORIGINALITY ANGST EMOTIONS DIALOGUE ACTION WIT BANTER SEX SCENES
SETTING DETAIL CONFLICT BACKSTORY

❑ REVIEWED?

152

Title:

AUTHOR:

DATE STARTED

SERIES/GENRE:

DATE FINISHED

EBOOK PAPER AUDIO

MY RATING

GREAT: CHARACTERS PLOT SUSPENSE DRAMA HUMOR HEROINE HERO
ORIGINALITY ANGST EMOTIONS DIALOGUE ACTION WIT BANTER SEX SCENES
SETTING DETAIL CONFLICT BACKSTORY

❑ REVIEWED?

Title:

AUTHOR:

SERIES/GENRE:

DATE STARTED

DATE FINISHED

EBOOK PAPER AUDIO

MY RATING

❑ REVIEWED?

GREAT: CHARACTERS PLOT SUSPENSE DRAMA HUMOR HEROINE HERO ORIGINALITY ANGST EMOTIONS DIALOGUE ACTION WIT BANTER SEX SCENES SETTING DETAIL CONFLICT BACKSTORY

Title:

AUTHOR:

SERIES/GENRE:

DATE STARTED

DATE FINISHED

EBOOK PAPER AUDIO

MY RATING

❑ REVIEWED?

GREAT: CHARACTERS PLOT SUSPENSE DRAMA HUMOR HEROINE HERO ORIGINALITY ANGST EMOTIONS DIALOGUE ACTION WIT BANTER SEX SCENES SETTING DETAIL CONFLICT BACKSTORY

155

Title:

AUTHOR:

SERIES/GENRE:

DATE STARTED

DATE FINISHED

EBOOK PAPER AUDIO

MY RATING

GREAT: CHARACTERS PLOT SUSPENSE DRAMA HUMOR HEROINE HERO ORIGINALITY ANGST EMOTIONS DIALOGUE ACTION WIT BANTER SEX SCENES SETTING DETAIL CONFLICT BACKSTORY

❑ REVIEWED?

156

Title:

AUTHOR:

SERIES/GENRE:

DATE STARTED

DATE FINISHED

EBOOK PAPER AUDIO

MY RATING

GREAT: CHARACTERS PLOT SUSPENSE DRAMA HUMOR HEROINE HERO ORIGINALITY ANGST EMOTIONS DIALOGUE ACTION WIT BANTER SEX SCENES SETTING DETAIL CONFLICT BACKSTORY

❑ REVIEWED?

Title:

AUTHOR:

DATE STARTED

SERIES/GENRE:

DATE FINISHED

EBOOK PAPER AUDIO

MY RATING

GREAT: CHARACTERS PLOT SUSPENSE DRAMA HUMOR HEROINE HERO ORIGINALITY ANGST EMOTIONS DIALOGUE ACTION WIT BANTER SEX SCENES SETTING DETAIL CONFLICT BACKSTORY

❑ REVIEWED?

Title:

AUTHOR:

DATE STARTED

SERIES/GENRE:

DATE FINISHED

EBOOK PAPER AUDIO

MY RATING

GREAT: CHARACTERS PLOT SUSPENSE DRAMA HUMOR HEROINE HERO ORIGINALITY ANGST EMOTIONS DIALOGUE ACTION WIT BANTER SEX SCENES SETTING DETAIL CONFLICT BACKSTORY

❑ REVIEWED?

“The essence of romance is uncertainty.”

OSCAR WILDE

159

Title:

AUTHOR:

SERIES/GENRE:

DATE STARTED

DATE FINISHED

EBOOK PAPER AUDIO

MY RATING

☆☆☆☆☆

❑ REVIEWED?

GREAT: CHARACTERS PLOT SUSPENSE DRAMA HUMOR HEROINE HERO ORIGINALITY ANGST EMOTIONS DIALOGUE ACTION WIT BANTER SEX SCENES SETTING DETAIL CONFLICT BACKSTORY

160

Title:

AUTHOR:

SERIES/GENRE:

DATE STARTED

DATE FINISHED

EBOOK PAPER AUDIO

MY RATING

☆☆☆☆☆

❑ REVIEWED?

GREAT: CHARACTERS PLOT SUSPENSE DRAMA HUMOR HEROINE HERO ORIGINALITY ANGST EMOTIONS DIALOGUE ACTION WIT BANTER SEX SCENES SETTING DETAIL CONFLICT BACKSTORY

Title:

AUTHOR:

DATE STARTED

SERIES/GENRE:

DATE FINISHED

EBOOK PAPER AUDIO

MY RATING

☐ REVIEWED?

GREAT: CHARACTERS PLOT SUSPENSE DRAMA HUMOR HEROINE HERO ORIGINALITY ANGST EMOTIONS DIALOGUE ACTION WIT BANTER SEX SCENES SETTING DETAIL CONFLICT BACKSTORY

Title:

AUTHOR:

DATE STARTED

SERIES/GENRE:

DATE FINISHED

EBOOK PAPER AUDIO

MY RATING

GREAT: CHARACTERS PLOT SUSPENSE DRAMA HUMOR HEROINE HERO ORIGINALITY ANGST EMOTIONS DIALOGUE ACTION WIT BANTER SEX SCENES SETTING DETAIL CONFLICT BACKSTORY

☐ REVIEWED?

Title:

AUTHOR:

DATE STARTED

/ /

SERIES/GENRE:

DATE FINISHED

/ /

EBOOK PAPER AUDIO

MY RATING

GREAT: CHARACTERS PLOT SUSPENSE DRAMA HUMOR HEROINE HERO ORIGINALITY ANGST EMOTIONS DIALOGUE ACTION WIT BANTER SEX SCENES SETTING DETAIL CONFLICT BACKSTORY

❑ REVIEWED?

Title:

AUTHOR:

DATE STARTED

/ /

SERIES/GENRE:

DATE FINISHED

/ /

EBOOK PAPER AUDIO

MY RATING

GREAT: CHARACTERS PLOT SUSPENSE DRAMA HUMOR HEROINE HERO ORIGINALITY ANGST EMOTIONS DIALOGUE ACTION WIT BANTER SEX SCENES SETTING DETAIL CONFLICT BACKSTORY

❑ REVIEWED?

165

Title:

AUTHOR:

SERIES/GENRE:

DATE STARTED

DATE FINISHED

EBOOK PAPER AUDIO

MY RATING

❑ REVIEWED?

GREAT: CHARACTERS PLOT SUSPENSE DRAMA HUMOR HEROINE HERO ORIGINALITY ANGST EMOTIONS DIALOGUE ACTION WIT BANTER SEX SCENES SETTING DETAIL CONFLICT BACKSTORY

166

Title:

AUTHOR:

SERIES/GENRE:

DATE STARTED

DATE FINISHED

EBOOK PAPER AUDIO

MY RATING

❑ REVIEWED?

GREAT: CHARACTERS PLOT SUSPENSE DRAMA HUMOR HEROINE HERO ORIGINALITY ANGST EMOTIONS DIALOGUE ACTION WIT BANTER SEX SCENES SETTING DETAIL CONFLICT BACKSTORY

Title:

AUTHOR:

DATE STARTED

SERIES/GENRE:

DATE FINISHED

EBOOK PAPER AUDIO

MY RATING

GREAT: CHARACTERS PLOT SUSPENSE DRAMA HUMOR HEROINE HERO ORIGINALITY ANGST EMOTIONS DIALOGUE ACTION WIT BANTER SEX SCENES SETTING DETAIL CONFLICT BACKSTORY

❑ REVIEWED?

Title:

AUTHOR:

DATE STARTED

SERIES/GENRE:

DATE FINISHED

EBOOK PAPER AUDIO

MY RATING

GREAT: CHARACTERS PLOT SUSPENSE DRAMA HUMOR HEROINE HERO ORIGINALITY ANGST EMOTIONS DIALOGUE ACTION WIT BANTER SEX SCENES SETTING DETAIL CONFLICT BACKSTORY

❑ REVIEWED?

169 Title:

AUTHOR:

DATE STARTED

SERIES/GENRE:

DATE FINISHED

EBOOK PAPER AUDIO

MY RATING

GREAT: CHARACTERS PLOT SUSPENSE DRAMA HUMOR HEROINE HERO ORIGINALITY ANGST EMOTIONS DIALOGUE ACTION WIT BANTER SEX SCENES SETTING DETAIL CONFLICT BACKSTORY

❑ REVIEWED?

170 Title:

AUTHOR:

DATE STARTED

SERIES/GENRE:

DATE FINISHED

EBOOK PAPER AUDIO

MY RATING

GREAT: CHARACTERS PLOT SUSPENSE DRAMA HUMOR HEROINE HERO ORIGINALITY ANGST EMOTIONS DIALOGUE ACTION WIT BANTER SEX SCENES SETTING DETAIL CONFLICT BACKSTORY

❑ REVIEWED?

Title:

AUTHOR:

SERIES/GENRE:

DATE STARTED

DATE FINISHED

EBOOK PAPER AUDIO

MY RATING

❏ REVIEWED?

GREAT: CHARACTERS PLOT SUSPENSE DRAMA HUMOR HEROINE HERO ORIGINALITY ANGST EMOTIONS DIALOGUE ACTION WIT BANTER SEX SCENES SETTING DETAIL CONFLICT BACKSTORY

172

Title:

AUTHOR:

SERIES/GENRE:

DATE STARTED

DATE FINISHED

EBOOK PAPER AUDIO

MY RATING

❏ REVIEWED?

GREAT: CHARACTERS PLOT SUSPENSE DRAMA HUMOR HEROINE HERO ORIGINALITY ANGST EMOTIONS DIALOGUE ACTION WIT BANTER SEX SCENES SETTING DETAIL CONFLICT BACKSTORY

Title:

AUTHOR:

DATE STARTED

SERIES/GENRE:

DATE FINISHED

EBOOK PAPER AUDIO

MY RATING

GREAT: CHARACTERS PLOT SUSPENSE DRAMA HUMOR HEROINE HERO ORIGINALITY ANGST EMOTIONS DIALOGUE ACTION WIT BANTER SEX SCENES SETTING DETAIL CONFLICT BACKSTORY

❑ REVIEWED?

Title:

AUTHOR:

DATE STARTED

SERIES/GENRE:

DATE FINISHED

EBOOK PAPER AUDIO

MY RATING

GREAT: CHARACTERS PLOT SUSPENSE DRAMA HUMOR HEROINE HERO ORIGINALITY ANGST EMOTIONS DIALOGUE ACTION WIT BANTER SEX SCENES SETTING DETAIL CONFLICT BACKSTORY

❑ REVIEWED?

Title:

AUTHOR:

SERIES/GENRE:

DATE STARTED

DATE FINISHED

EBOOK PAPER AUDIO

MY RATING

❑ REVIEWED?

GREAT: CHARACTERS PLOT SUSPENSE DRAMA HUMOR HEROINE HERO ORIGINALITY ANGST EMOTIONS DIALOGUE ACTION WIT BANTER SEX SCENES SETTING DETAIL CONFLICT BACKSTORY

Title:

AUTHOR:

SERIES/GENRE:

DATE STARTED

DATE FINISHED

EBOOK PAPER AUDIO

MY RATING

❑ REVIEWED?

GREAT: CHARACTERS PLOT SUSPENSE DRAMA HUMOR HEROINE HERO ORIGINALITY ANGST EMOTIONS DIALOGUE ACTION WIT BANTER SEX SCENES SETTING DETAIL CONFLICT BACKSTORY

Title:

AUTHOR:

SERIES/GENRE:

DATE STARTED

DATE FINISHED

EBOOK PAPER AUDIO

MY RATING

GREAT: CHARACTERS PLOT SUSPENSE DRAMA HUMOR HEROINE HERO ORIGINALITY ANGST EMOTIONS DIALOGUE ACTION WIT BANTER SEX SCENES SETTING DETAIL CONFLICT BACKSTORY

❏ REVIEWED?

178

Title:

AUTHOR:

SERIES/GENRE:

DATE STARTED

DATE FINISHED

EBOOK PAPER AUDIO

MY RATING

GREAT: CHARACTERS PLOT SUSPENSE DRAMA HUMOR HEROINE HERO ORIGINALITY ANGST EMOTIONS DIALOGUE ACTION WIT BANTER SEX SCENES SETTING DETAIL CONFLICT BACKSTORY

❏ REVIEWED?

Title:

AUTHOR:

SERIES/GENRE:

DATE STARTED

DATE FINISHED

EBOOK PAPER AUDIO

MY RATING

❑ REVIEWED?

GREAT: CHARACTERS PLOT SUSPENSE DRAMA HUMOR HEROINE HERO ORIGINALITY ANGST EMOTIONS DIALOGUE ACTION WIT BANTER SEX SCENES SETTING DETAIL CONFLICT BACKSTORY

Title:

AUTHOR:

SERIES/GENRE:

DATE STARTED

DATE FINISHED

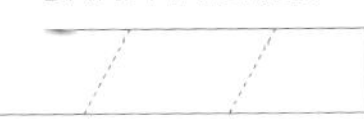

EBOOK PAPER AUDIO

MY RATING

❑ REVIEWED?

GREAT: CHARACTERS PLOT SUSPENSE DRAMA HUMOR HEROINE HERO ORIGINALITY ANGST EMOTIONS DIALOGUE ACTION WIT BANTER SEX SCENES SETTING DETAIL CONFLICT BACKSTORY

181

Title:

AUTHOR:

SERIES/GENRE:

DATE STARTED

DATE FINISHED

EBOOK PAPER AUDIO

MY RATING

❑ REVIEWED?

GREAT: CHARACTERS PLOT SUSPENSE DRAMA HUMOR HEROINE HERO ORIGINALITY ANGST EMOTIONS DIALOGUE ACTION WIT BANTER SEX SCENES SETTING DETAIL CONFLICT BACKSTORY

182

Title:

AUTHOR:

SERIES/GENRE:

DATE STARTED

DATE FINISHED

EBOOK PAPER AUDIO

MY RATING

❑ REVIEWED?

GREAT: CHARACTERS PLOT SUSPENSE DRAMA HUMOR HEROINE HERO ORIGINALITY ANGST EMOTIONS DIALOGUE ACTION WIT BANTER SEX SCENES SETTING DETAIL CONFLICT BACKSTORY

183

Title:

AUTHOR:

SERIES/GENRE:

DATE STARTED

DATE FINISHED

EBOOK PAPER AUDIO

MY RATING

GREAT: CHARACTERS PLOT SUSPENSE DRAMA HUMOR HEROINE HERO ORIGINALITY ANGST EMOTIONS DIALOGUE ACTION WIT BANTER SEX SCENES SETTING DETAIL CONFLICT BACKSTORY

❏ REVIEWED?

184

Title:

AUTHOR:

SERIES/GENRE:

DATE STARTED

DATE FINISHED

EBOOK PAPER AUDIO

MY RATING

GREAT: CHARACTERS PLOT SUSPENSE DRAMA HUMOR HEROINE HERO ORIGINALITY ANGST EMOTIONS DIALOGUE ACTION WIT BANTER SEX SCENES SETTING DETAIL CONFLICT BACKSTORY

❏ REVIEWED?

Title:

AUTHOR:

DATE STARTED

SERIES/GENRE:

DATE FINISHED

EBOOK PAPER AUDIO

MY RATING

GREAT: CHARACTERS PLOT SUSPENSE DRAMA HUMOR HEROINE HERO ORIGINALITY ANGST EMOTIONS DIALOGUE ACTION WIT BANTER SEX SCENES SETTING DETAIL CONFLICT BACKSTORY

❑ REVIEWED?

186

Title:

AUTHOR:

DATE STARTED

SERIES/GENRE:

DATE FINISHED

EBOOK PAPER AUDIO

MY RATING

GREAT: CHARACTERS PLOT SUSPENSE DRAMA HUMOR HEROINE HERO ORIGINALITY ANGST EMOTIONS DIALOGUE ACTION WIT BANTER SEX SCENES SETTING DETAIL CONFLICT BACKSTORY

❑ REVIEWED?

Title:

AUTHOR:

SERIES/GENRE:

DATE STARTED

/ /

DATE FINISHED

/ /

EBOOK PAPER AUDIO

MY RATING

❑ REVIEWED?

GREAT: CHARACTERS PLOT SUSPENSE DRAMA HUMOR HEROINE HERO ORIGINALITY ANGST EMOTIONS DIALOGUE ACTION WIT BANTER SEX SCENES SETTING DETAIL CONFLICT BACKSTORY

Title:

AUTHOR:

SERIES/GENRE:

DATE STARTED

/ /

DATE FINISHED

/ /

EBOOK PAPER AUDIO

MY RATING

❑ REVIEWED?

GREAT: CHARACTERS PLOT SUSPENSE DRAMA HUMOR HEROINE HERO ORIGINALITY ANGST EMOTIONS DIALOGUE ACTION WIT BANTER SEX SCENES SETTING DETAIL CONFLICT BACKSTORY

189

Title:

AUTHOR:

SERIES/GENRE:

DATE STARTED

DATE FINISHED

EBOOK PAPER AUDIO

MY RATING

❑ REVIEWED?

GREAT: CHARACTERS PLOT SUSPENSE DRAMA HUMOR HEROINE HERO ORIGINALITY ANGST EMOTIONS DIALOGUE ACTION WIT BANTER SEX SCENES SETTING DETAIL CONFLICT BACKSTORY

190

Title:

AUTHOR:

SERIES/GENRE:

DATE STARTED

DATE FINISHED

EBOOK PAPER AUDIO

MY RATING

❑ REVIEWED?

GREAT: CHARACTERS PLOT SUSPENSE DRAMA HUMOR HEROINE HERO ORIGINALITY ANGST EMOTIONS DIALOGUE ACTION WIT BANTER SEX SCENES SETTING DETAIL CONFLICT BACKSTORY

Title:

AUTHOR:

SERIES/GENRE:

DATE STARTED

DATE FINISHED

EBOOK PAPER AUDIO

MY RATING

❑ REVIEWED?

GREAT: CHARACTERS PLOT SUSPENSE DRAMA HUMOR HEROINE HERO ORIGINALITY ANGST EMOTIONS DIALOGUE ACTION WIT BANTER SEX SCENES SETTING DETAIL CONFLICT BACKSTORY

Title:

AUTHOR:

SERIES/GENRE:

DATE STARTED

DATE FINISHED

EBOOK PAPER AUDIO

MY RATING

❑ REVIEWED?

GREAT: CHARACTERS PLOT SUSPENSE DRAMA HUMOR HEROINE HERO ORIGINALITY ANGST EMOTIONS DIALOGUE ACTION WIT BANTER SEX SCENES SETTING DETAIL CONFLICT BACKSTORY

Title:

AUTHOR:

SERIES/GENRE:

DATE STARTED

DATE FINISHED

EBOOK PAPER AUDIO

MY RATING

❑ REVIEWED?

GREAT: CHARACTERS PLOT SUSPENSE DRAMA HUMOR HEROINE HERO ORIGINALITY ANGST EMOTIONS DIALOGUE ACTION WIT BANTER SEX SCENES SETTING DETAIL CONFLICT BACKSTORY

Title:

AUTHOR:

SERIES/GENRE:

DATE STARTED

DATE FINISHED

EBOOK PAPER AUDIO

MY RATING

❑ REVIEWED?

GREAT: CHARACTERS PLOT SUSPENSE DRAMA HUMOR HEROINE HERO ORIGINALITY ANGST EMOTIONS DIALOGUE ACTION WIT BANTER SEX SCENES SETTING DETAIL CONFLICT BACKSTORY

Title:

AUTHOR: ______________________

SERIES/GENRE: ______________________

DATE STARTED

DATE FINISHED

EBOOK PAPER AUDIO

MY RATING

GREAT: CHARACTERS PLOT SUSPENSE DRAMA HUMOR HEROINE HERO ORIGINALITY ANGST EMOTIONS DIALOGUE ACTION WIT BANTER SEX SCENES SETTING DETAIL CONFLICT BACKSTORY

❑ REVIEWED?

Title:

AUTHOR: ______________________

SERIES/GENRE: ______________________

DATE STARTED

DATE FINISHED

EBOOK PAPER AUDIO

MY RATING

GREAT: CHARACTERS PLOT SUSPENSE DRAMA HUMOR HEROINE HERO ORIGINALITY ANGST EMOTIONS DIALOGUE ACTION WIT BANTER SEX SCENES SETTING DETAIL CONFLICT BACKSTORY

❑ REVIEWED?

Title:

AUTHOR: ______________________

SERIES/GENRE: ______________________

DATE STARTED

DATE FINISHED

EBOOK PAPER AUDIO

MY RATING

❑ REVIEWED?

GREAT: CHARACTERS PLOT SUSPENSE DRAMA HUMOR HEROINE HERO ORIGINALITY ANGST EMOTIONS DIALOGUE ACTION WIT BANTER SEX SCENES SETTING DETAIL CONFLICT BACKSTORY

Title:

AUTHOR: ______________________

SERIES/GENRE: ______________________

DATE STARTED

DATE FINISHED

EBOOK PAPER AUDIO

MY RATING

❑ REVIEWED?

GREAT: CHARACTERS PLOT SUSPENSE DRAMA HUMOR HEROINE HERO ORIGINALITY ANGST EMOTIONS DIALOGUE ACTION WIT BANTER SEX SCENES SETTING DETAIL CONFLICT BACKSTORY

Title:

AUTHOR:

SERIES/GENRE:

DATE STARTED

DATE FINISHED

EBOOK PAPER AUDIO

MY RATING

GREAT: CHARACTERS PLOT SUSPENSE DRAMA HUMOR HEROINE HERO ORIGINALITY ANGST EMOTIONS DIALOGUE ACTION WIT BANTER SEX SCENES SETTING DETAIL CONFLICT BACKSTORY

❑ REVIEWED?

Title:

AUTHOR:

SERIES/GENRE:

DATE STARTED

DATE FINISHED

EBOOK PAPER AUDIO

MY RATING

GREAT: CHARACTERS PLOT SUSPENSE DRAMA HUMOR HEROINE HERO ORIGINALITY ANGST EMOTIONS DIALOGUE ACTION WIT BANTER SEX SCENES SETTING DETAIL CONFLICT BACKSTORY

❑ REVIEWED?

“She read books as one would breathe air, to fill up and live.”

ANNIE DILLARD